ABRAHAM LINCOLN

Troll Associates

ABRAHAM LINCOLN

by Rae Bains

Illustrated by Dick Smolinski

Troll Associates

Library of Congress Cataloging in Publication Data

Bains, Rae.
    Abraham Lincoln.

    Summary: A biography of the sixteenth president, known
as a wise and compassionate man and an eloquent speaker,
whose determination helped preserve the Union during the
Civil War.
    1. Lincoln, Abraham, 1809-1865—Juvenile literature.
2. Presidents—United States—Biography—Juvenile
literature. [1. Lincoln, Abraham, 1809-1865. 2. Presi-
dents] I. Smolinski, Dick, ill. II. Title.
E457.905.B23   1985   973.7'092'4 [B] [92]   84-2581
ISBN 0-8167-0146-6 (lib. bdg.)
ISBN 0-8167-0147-4 (pbk.)

Abraham Lincoln, the sixteenth President of the United States, rose from humble beginnings to the nation's highest office. He was always straightforward, wise, and compassionate. Though he had little formal schooling, he became a well-educated man and an eloquent speaker. His strong will and great determination helped preserve the Union during the long and bitter Civil War.

The second child of Tom and Nancy Lincoln, Abraham Lincoln was born in the Kentucky territory on February 12, 1809. Sinking Springs Farm was Abraham's home for the first two years of his life. Then his family moved to Knob Creek, about ten miles away.

In the five years the Lincolns lived there, Abe learned to farm, fish, read, and write. He had less than one year of schooling. Part of it was at Zachariah Riney's one-room schoolhouse, a couple of miles from the Knob Creek farm. It didn't take long for the bright young boy to learn writing, reading, and basic arithmetic.

When Abe was seven years old, the Lincolns moved across the Ohio River into Indiana. They settled at Pigeon Creek, on one hundred sixty acres of uncleared land. It was a rough, harsh life.

In later years, when Lincoln was running for political office, his political enemies mocked him because of his humble beginnings. They meant to insult him. But Lincoln responded with laughter and with pride in his background. He was proud of having

helped his father build a house and make furniture. He was proud of having earned money by splitting rails as a young man. He believed in honest, hard labor. And he believed that most Americans would respect him for it.

In the fall of 1818, when Abe was nine years old, his mother died. It was a crushing blow to the boy, to his eleven-year-old sister, Sarah, and to the children's father. For a year, the cabin on Pigeon Creek was a sad and lonely place. Then Mr. Lincoln remarried.

The new Mrs. Lincoln—Sarah Johnston— believed that young Abraham was going to be a great man someday. She insisted that he be educated. And so, whenever the school near Pigeon Creek was open, she encouraged Abe to go.

As a teenager, Abe Lincoln read every book he could get his hands on. Once he walked twenty miles to borrow a book. Another time, a book he borrowed was damaged by rain. To pay for the damage, Abe worked three days for the farmer who owned the book. Abe had a strong sense of responsibility and honesty.

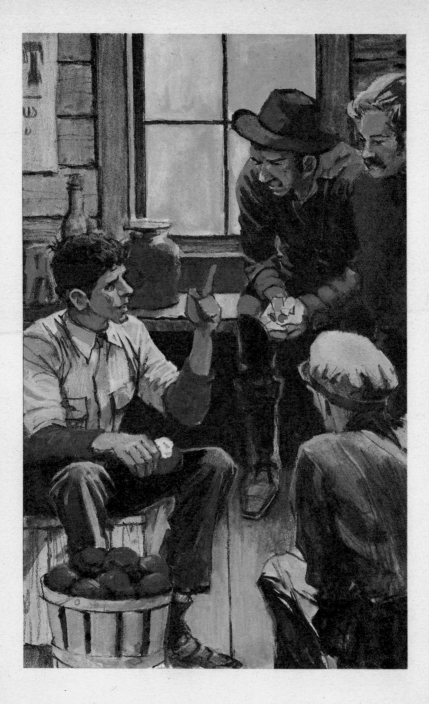

During his teen years, Lincoln developed a great talent for public speaking. He often walked down the road to James Gentry's village store. Neighborhood people often gathered there to tell stories and to exchange gossip. This was the chief form of entertainment in rural areas at that time. Abe, who had been shy as a child, blossomed at storytelling in Gentry's store. He was soon considered one of the best talkers in the area.

In 1830, when Abe was twenty-one, the Lincolns moved again and settled in Illinois. Abe stayed with his family for a year. This was long enough to help build a cabin, plant the first year's crop, and split rails for fencing. The next year, he took off on his own for the first time. He worked on a flatboat going to New Orleans.

When Abe returned to Illinois, he went to work as a clerk in a general store. The store was in New Salem, Illinois, which was to be Lincoln's home for the next six years. During that time, he served for three months in the Illinois militia, where he was elected captain by his fellow militiamen. Many years later, he said that being chosen captain gave him greater pleasure than any other honor or distinction bestowed upon him.

Shortly after serving in the militia, Abe
ran for the Illinois legislature, but was
defeated. Then he ran a general store for a
few months, but the store did not do well.
The following year, he was appointed New
Salem's postmaster. And the year after that,
in 1834, Lincoln was successful in his bid for
election to the Illinois state legislature.

He served for eight years—four two-year terms—as a member of the legislature. At the same time, he ran a general store. But he wasn't a very good businessman, and again the store did not do well.

While serving in the state legislature, Lincoln studied law. In 1837, he became an attorney, licensed to practice in the state of Illinois. A few years after that, he married Mary Todd.

For twenty-four years, Lincoln practiced law in Springfield, the state capital. He enjoyed a reputation as one of the state's best trial lawyers. In time, he earned a very good income, which enabled him, his wife, and their three sons to live in a large, comfortable home. The years in Springfield were among the happiest of his life.

But concern about important issues of the time drew Lincoln from his secure world into national politics. Slavery was one of these issues. Would the new territories of the American West be admitted to the Union as free states or slave states? The future of the United States depended on the answer to that question.

Abraham Lincoln had always believed that slavery was morally wrong. However, he did not believe that slavery should be abolished in those states where it had existed since the country was founded. Lincoln felt this way because he was certain that an attempt to end slavery in the South would cause a split in the Union. And he believed that the Union must be preserved at all costs.

Lincoln was equally firm, however, in his belief that slavery should not be extended into the western territories. In other words, Lincoln did not set out to eliminate slavery, but rather to keep it from spreading.

After serving in the United States House of Representatives, Lincoln ran for the U.S. Senate in 1858. His opponent was Stephen A. Douglas, who was not against slavery. During the campaign, the two candidates faced each other in a series of public debates. Although Douglas won the election, the debates made Lincoln a nationally known figure.

His reputation was so impressive that the newly organized Republican Party chose him as their 1860 nominee for President. When the voting was done, Abraham Lincoln had been elected the sixteenth President of the United States.

Between the election, in November of 1860, and the inauguration, in March of 1861, the Union began to come apart. In December 1860, South Carolina seceded from the United States. It was quickly followed by the other southern states. Together they formed the Confederate States of America.

Then, on April 12, 1861, Confederate soldiers attacked Fort Sumter, a Union garrison in Charleston, South Carolina. The Civil War had begun.

For four years the Union and Confederacy fought the bloodiest, most devastating war in American history. As the President, Lincoln wanted only to end the war and preserve the Union. In 1862, he wrote, "My paramount object in this struggle is to save the Union, and is not either to save or destroy slavery."

But soon afterward, he had changed his policy toward slavery. He issued the Emancipation Proclamation, which stated that all slaves in states that were still in

rebellion on January 1, 1863, would be set free. The slaves in states loyal to the Union were not freed, and the federal government could not enforce the Emancipation Proclamation in the Confederate States.

Although any southern state that was willing to return to the Union would have been welcomed back, even as a slave state, the South refused to give in. The war raged on, and the move to end slavery entirely was strengthened.

In November 1863, President Lincoln made his memorable Gettysburg Address. The occasion was the dedication of the cemetery for the soldiers who had fallen in battle at Gettysburg, Pennsylvania, five months earlier.

In his speech, Lincoln spoke of all the dead soldiers, saying, "we here highly resolve that these dead shall not have died in vain—that this nation, under God, shall have a new birth of freedom—and that government of the people, by the people, for the people, shall not perish from the earth."

Lincoln repeated this theme at the inauguration following his re-election as President in 1864. It was clear that the war was coming to a close and that the North would be victorious.

But Lincoln, a just and merciful man, was not elated by the victory. Rather, he was saddened by the four years of death and suffering on both sides. And with the hope of binding up the nation's wounds, he asked for charity for all and malice toward none.

On April 9, 1865, General Robert E. Lee, commander of the Confederate Army, surrendered to General Ulysses S. Grant, commander of the Union troops. The war was over, but there was still much to be done. Abraham Lincoln had preserved the nation. However, he did not live to lead it through times of peace.

On April 14, 1865, as President and Mrs. Lincoln attended the performance of a play, tragedy struck. As the Lincolns sat in the presidential box at Ford's Theater in Washington, D.C., a shot echoed through the theater. John Wilkes Booth, an actor who sympathized with the southern cause, had shot Lincoln in the head.

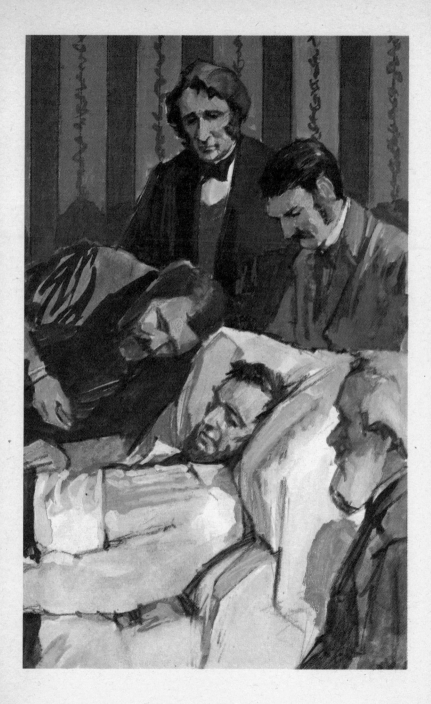

The President was carried to a house across the street, where he died the next morning. The whole nation was in shock. Abraham Lincoln, the man of the people, would be deeply missed by his fellow Americans in the days to come. But his goodness, honesty, and compassion would be remembered forever.